A HOPE AND A FUTURE
God's Provision in Difficult Times

GRAHAM

ORIGINAL PUBLICATION

© Copyright 2002 • Moody Press

All rights reserved

Printed in the United States of America

REVISED PUBLICATION

2015–PowerPoint Ministries, LLC

All rights reserved

Original Publication--Library of Congress Cataloging-in-Publication Data

Graham, Jack, 1950 – A Hope and A Future: God's Provision for Difficult Times/ Jack Graham.

p. cm.

ISBN 0-8024-6492-0

1. Consolation. 2. Providence and government of God. 3. Christian life—Baptist authors. I. Title.

BV4905.3 .G78 2002

248.8'6 -- dc21

2002020832

*Blessed be the God and Father of our
Lord Jesus Christ! According to his great mercy,
he has caused us to be born again to a living hope through
the resurrection of Jesus Christ from the dead, to an
inheritance that is imperishable, undefiled,
and unfading, kept in heaven for you...*
—1 Peter 1:3–4

JACK GRAHAM

───◇───

CONTENTS

INTRODUCTION

Access to Hope

It is said that a Union soldier, during the throes of the American Civil War, tried repeatedly to see President Lincoln at the White House in Washington, D.C. The president's staff turned away the soldier each time he asked for a meeting, saying the president was too busy to see him. Supposedly, the president's young son, Tad, encountered the soldier in the halls of the White House and asked him why he looked so sad. Upon hearing the soldier's story of troubles back home, Tad offered to help. "What can *you* do?" the soldier asked, not knowing who the boy was. Without a word, Tad Lincoln took the soldier's hand and led him through the corridors, past the White House staff, and into the Oval Office. "Father," Tad said, "this soldier needs your help." Who your daddy is makes all the difference in times of great need.

I don't know how this book has found its way into your hands. You could be browsing through it at a bookstore, or perhaps you received it as a gift and are paging through it out of curiosity. Although I trust this book will be an encouragement to all who read it, I wrote it for a particular kind of person—those whose tears stained the cover before ever getting to the first page; the person who read the word *hope* in the title the way a condemned man would read a pardon; the person for whom the world has become a whirl without end.

You may be like the Union soldier whose world had fallen apart during a time of great trouble and testing. But one thing sets you drastically apart from him: You will never have trouble getting an appointment with the one Person who can give you hope. Your Father in heaven will see you and hear your story, any time of the day or night. If your life has become a battlefield of conflicting emotions, broken relationships, unfocused days, and sleepless nights, you need to be reminded: You have a Father who knows your needs and wants to walk and talk through these days with you. That is why I have written this book—to remind the child of God what is true when nothing makes sense.

> *For you did not receive the spirit of slavery to fall back into fear, but you have received the Spirit of adoption as sons, by whom we cry, "Abba! Father!" The Spirit himself bears witness with our spirit that we are children of God, and if children, then heirs—heirs of God and fellow heirs with Christ, provided we suffer with him in order that we may also be glorified with him* (Romans 8:15–17).

The apostle Paul wrote a letter to some Christians in Rome for whom life was confusing at best and life threatening at worst. They needed a sense of the big picture, to understand the *whys* and *wherefores* of what they were going through. There was no love lost between the Jewish and Gentile Christians in the Church— neither could figure out why God had saved the other. But beyond that, the whole Church was constantly in danger of being squashed by the heavy heel of the Roman boot. The Roman government had grown weary of the "Christ movement" ever since the Nazarene carpenter named Jesus turned the Judean province into a hotbed of religious discontent. Their patience with Christians in Rome could run out at any minute.

So why did God allow them (and us) to experience such difficult times? Why, in other words, would God save us to suffer? That was the Roman Christians' question—and it is probably a question you have asked, or are asking yourself. Paul gives the answer in Romans, chapter 8. God didn't save you to suffer, Paul says. He saved you to make you His child and heir; to make you the eternal brothers and sisters of the Lord Jesus Christ.

And just as Jesus trusted His heavenly Father, even in suffering, you must learn to trust Him too.

Paul says God is our "Abba"—our papa, or daddy. Many people today have grown up without a father in their home, much less a loving and accessible one. But that will never be true of you if you are a believer in Christ. I hope that as you read through these meditations on hope, you will sense the Holy Spirit Himself telling your spirit that you are a child of God, loved deeply by your heavenly Father. All the hope you will ever need is found in Him.

PART ONE

God Gives Us Perspective

"For I know the plans I have for you," declares the LORD, "plans to prosper you and not to harm you, plans to give you a hope and a future."
—Jeremiah 29:11

The American Dream has been dramatized and glamorized by the most creative of people. We all love to hear the stories of immigrants who came to our great nation and found unlimited opportunities for growth. Then there is the person who was born into poverty but worked hard and prospered greatly. I like to hear about people who had the courage and strength to take a risk and do something that most would say could never be done.

Oh, how we need Christians to pursue a dream much greater than the American Dream! The American Dream has become tarnished, and that is largely due to the perspective of the ones pursuing it. One dream will never tarnish and never disappoint anyone. In Ephesians 3:14–19, Paul is praying from a prison cell, and yet his spirit is free.

For this reason I bow my knees before the Father, from whom every family in heaven and on earth is named, that according to the riches of his glory he may grant you to be strengthened with power through his Spirit in your inner being, so that Christ may dwell in your hearts through faith—that you, being rooted and grounded in love, may have strength to comprehend with all the saints what is the breadth and length and height and depth, and to know the love of Christ that surpasses knowledge, that you may be filled with all the fullness of God.

The next two verses reveal why Paul could pray for the

saints at Ephesus the way he did:

> *Now to him who is able to do far more abundantly than all that we ask or think, according to the power at work within us, to him be glory in the church and in Christ Jesus throughout all generations, forever and ever. Amen.*

That is incredibly insightful perspective from Paul.

We cannot expect God to provide for us abundantly unless we are willing to bow before Him in believing, confident, dependent prayer. Paul's prayer reveals his perspective clearly. Paul had been transformed by the grace of God, and his prayer is filled with wonder, love, and praise. We have unlimited possibilities when we realize whom we serve.

A STEADFAST FOCUS

It concerns me when I read articles describing the future of the Church in which churchgoers are defined as the "consumer." The surveys taken identify what the "consumer" wants or needs. We must get a different perspective on what the Church is all about. We are not consumers; we exist for the pleasure and the glory of God. When we live for Him, we are promised His power. The word *power* that Paul uses means energy—dynamic, life-giving energy. Do your friends know that this incomparable power is at work in you?

The power that works in the believer is the same power that raised Jesus Christ from the dead. It is the same power that exalted Jesus above the heavens and the earth and subjected everything under His feet—all principalities, good and bad. *That is* the power that lives in us!

Mankind has two great enemies: death and evil. By the power of His Resurrection, Jesus Christ has overcome death, and by the power of His exaltation, He has overcome evil. And one day He will banish evil from the face of the universe. Can you keep that in perspective when you face the death of a dream?

So many Christians today are just *enduring* the Christian life rather than *enjoying* the Christian life in power and victory. So many Christians' lives are characterized by frustration and failure, defeat and disillusionment. They may know their sins are forgiven and they may be certain they're going to heaven one day, but life in the *here and now* is spiritually neutral.

When we live a truly Christ-centered life, we will not live focused on what we need or what we want to do. We do not need to be victims of sin and temptation. We do not need to live self-absorbed, egocentric lives but instead lives that are full and release the very Spirit and the power of God. Our perspective of God is just too limited. Keep your focus on Him and His power.

A STRONG FAITH

Remember in his prayer, Paul proclaims that God is able to do more than we could ask or think—and not only is He able to do *all that we ask* or think, He is able to do *all that we dare not ask.* More ... much more ... far more ... exceedingly more! We cannot expect too much from God.

Paul is not giving us a false hope. He knew the source of his faith. Remember, Paul had witnessed the grace of God transform the pagans at Ephesus. Ephesus was dominated by false religion. It was intellectually sophisticated, as the cultural elite of the ancient world lived in Ephesus. If you were strategically planning to grow a church, Ephesus would not have been the prime location. Paul didn't organize a political campaign; he didn't picket; and he didn't convince everybody to protest. He took to the pulpit and proclaimed the message of Jesus Christ.

We know how important it is to affect and influence our culture for Christ, but our primary vision, our primary purpose, goal and mission, must be to proclaim the Gospel of Jesus Christ and to impact the culture by changing lives—one at a time. Let your faith be stretched. Revival *will* take place in America and we will impact the social structures of our culture when God's people pray and when God's people proclaim the Word of God. You must believe that God can change lives ... that He is able to save those who come to Him ... that He is able to transform lives.

Our faith must be stretched to look forward with hope. We live in tenuous times. Each day we're bombarded with images of war and famine, brutality and desperation. Life seems out of control. But God is able, and if we confess, "I am not able, Lord, but You are able," that will stretch our faith.

A SECURE FAITH

> *When we've been there ten thousand years*
> *Bright shining as the sun,*
> *We've no less days to sing God's praise*
> *Than when we first begun.*

"Amazing Grace" by John Newton
(final verse by unknown author)

We, the people of God, are destined for the throne. We are investing in that which is forever. The Church is important to God, and if there's ever going to be spiritual renewal or awakening in America and in the world, it will be because it happened in His Church. The future of America is in the hands of His Church because we possess the message of Christ. We possess the power of Christ, and we are in the heart of God forever.

GOD AND THE BOX TOP

I confess—I loved revealing some of life's big secrets to my children. (And now I enjoy doing the same with my grandchildren!) I'm talking about the serious stuff: how it's easier to blow up a balloon if you stretch it a few times; or how you twist cookies apart so you can eat the creamy stuff first. Big kids love to teach little kids the tricks of the trade!

For those who still enjoy family-time jigsaw puzzles, another great secret is showing children how much easier it is if you let the picture on the top of the box guide you. Find the four corner pieces, then all the pieces with straight edges, and the perimeter is done. Then look at the box top and begin grouping similarly-colored pieces together and, voilà, it's a piece of cake. If you're a puzzle purist who believes that using the picture to guide you is akin to using a calculator for math, forgive me. But there's a spiritual lesson in puzzles—especially for those who are suffering. From our perspective, life is an unfinished puzzle. But God sees the whole picture and knows exactly where each piece fits.

The Russian philosopher, novelist and historian, Aleksandr Solzhenitsyn, spent eight years in prison in the 1940s for negative remarks about Soviet leader Joseph Stalin. He won the Nobel Prize for Literature in 1970 for his writings, which exposed some of the Soviet Union's atrocities during the Stalinist period. However, when he was in prison, life was dark and filled with despair. Working on a chain gang in Siberia, he and other prisoners were made to labor most of the day without speaking. Though he had become a believer in Christ, the suffering he endured as a prisoner took its toll. He decided he could not go on, and he made plans to end his life.

With no weapon or tool with which to kill himself, he decided the best way to end his life was to pretend he was trying to escape. He knew the guards would open fire and shoot him—and that would end his suffering. On the day he planned to make his break for eternal freedom, he was hunched down, squatting on the ground, preparing to run. Just before leaping to his fate, a man came and stood beside him, a man he had never seen before and never saw again. A man, Solzhenitsyn later wrote, whose face shone like that of an angel.

The stranger bent down and, with a stick in his hand, drew a vertical line in the dirt, and then crossed it with a horizontal line—making the shape of the cross. Solzhenitsyn looked at the cross in the dirt, looked at the angelic face staring down at him, and suddenly was overwhelmed with the peace of God. He knew taking his life was not what he should do. "I chose to remain in the circumstances that I found myself, little realizing that less than a week later I would be in Geneva, a free man!" The eight years of Solzhenitsyn's horrible life in prison— suffering in the intellectual and geographic wasteland of Siberia—ended within seven days of the day he had planned to take his life. If Aleksandr Solzhenitsyn had only seen the *box top of his life*, he would have never planned to end it. He would have seen, "There! There is the day it ends, the day I will be free! I can make it until that day!" Knowing how the pieces of his life fit together would have given him hope. Knowing God was working things together for his good would have saved his life. Fortunately, God intervened miraculously and saved him in his hour of despair.

> *And we know that for those who love God all things work together for good, for those who are called according to his purpose* (Romans 8:28).

Today is only one small piece of the incomplete puzzle that is your life. And only God has the box top. Will you trust Him that today fits perfectly? As ill shaped and strange looking as it may seem, today has its place. God knows what the final image looks like, so allow Him to piece it together. The day you see the completed puzzle, you will be grateful for God's sovereign hand in it.

THE PRESENCE OF THE FUTURE

S ometimes a little hope can go a long way. It went all the way to the altar for a young couple I had the privilege of marrying—a couple for whom almost no one held out any hope. If the husband had not grasped the glimmer of hope God put in his heart, he and his wife would be single still.

The ceremony I officiated for this couple was actually the second for both of them. Like many today, both had been divorced. But unlike most, they were divorced from each other. They began married life as young attorneys on the fast track to success—or so they thought. They were making lots of money and lived in a beautiful, upscale house with a swimming pool and tennis court in the backyard—all the things that are supposed to make us happy. However, contrary to outward appearances, they were miserable and their marriage was a disaster. They took the easy way out, signing divorce papers and heading their separate ways.

But the husband—broken, discouraged and lost—found his way to a service at our church. Something said in that service sparked hope on the dry tinder of his heart—and a flame of faith burst forth. He left his seat and came forward and gave his life to Christ. Just like the Bible says, he became a new creation (2 Corinthians 5:17). And, for the first time, he had hope! He believed that all the suffering he and his wife had endured might have had a higher purpose. Slowly, he began to communicate with his ex-wife, telling her about the changes Christ was making in his life. Suspicious at first, she didn't join him at church until six months later—and his hope then became her hope! She became a new person in Christ as well.

And not only the creation, but we ourselves, who have

the firstfruits of the Spirit, groan inwardly as we wait eagerly for adoption as sons, the redemption of our bodies (Romans 8:23).

For the first time, this young couple now possessed hope that something bigger than their failures and frustrations was taking shape. They believed they now possessed not only a way to endure difficult times but a reason to endure them as well. So within a year, they joined hands in marriage for the second time before God and their friends. And it took place because hope was seized when it first made an appearance and not released until its fruit was borne.

Hope comes in different ways and at different times. But regardless of when or how it comes, hope always does the same thing. It offers the one who will take hold of it the prospect of a peaceful and fruitful future (Jeremiah 29:11). In the Old Testament, for instance, when the harvest started, gathered immediately were the firstfruits—the grains that first matured in the fields.

They were brought as an offering before the Lord out of gratitude for what the Israelites believed was yet to come—a bountiful harvest from the hand of God. On the day the firstfruits were gathered, the full harvest was just a hope, but a hope for which they held evidence in their hands. Hope translated to faith and faith to action as they sharpened their scythes and prepared to turn hope into harvest.

For the Israelite farmer, the first grains held out promise for the harvest. For the lost young lawyer, newfound faith held out promise for his marriage. And for you, if you are a believer in Christ, the Holy Spirit living in you holds out promise for your future. God gives us the Holy Spirit as the firstfruit, telling us the best is yet to come.

Hope is the reality that brings the *future* into the *present* by faith. Hope is the presence of the future. Hope is like an old-fashioned keyhole—a tiny opening through which you can see what awaits you on the other side. A farmer sees a harvest. A divorced husband sees a happy marriage. What do *you* see? The Holy Spirit is in you to give you hope. He is just a taste of what is to come. He is the presence of the future for you.

LIVING ON TIPTOES

Having traveled abroad a bit recently, I have grown accustomed at airports to seeing different types of "waiters"—people waiting to pick up someone arriving on an international flight. First, there are the "drivers." You can pick them out because they're holding up placards or electronic signs with the names of travelers. Drivers are at the airport to greet someone they don't know. For them, it's just a job to—"Pick up Mr. Smith and take him wherever he wants to go." Get a call, hold up a sign, deliver a person. Drivers are attentive, but you wouldn't say they're excited for the arrival of the person they're awaiting.

Then there are the "associates." They're at the airport to pick up people they know but whose arrival is also not an emotional event. Perhaps the person waiting at the airport is a business colleague or an intern. These people wait by reading magazines or playing games on their smart phones or chatting with other "associate" type waiters. They amble over at just the right time to greet their party. For them, waiting is a routine thing.

Finally, there are the "eagers." These are the folks who have perfected the art of waiting eagerly. If it's a young woman pacing back and forth with an anxious, almost teary-eyed look, I know it's a fiancée or a newlywed waiting on her knight in airborne armor to return from their first separation. If it's an older couple standing at the head of the line, I know it's grandparents waiting to smother a grandchild with kisses, or parents waiting for a globe-trotting student to come home after a way-too-long absence.

But the most fun "eagers" to watch are the little kids.

If they've come to pick up their daddy, they're racing back and forth; they're jumping up and down; they're embarrassing their mother with their shrieks: "Is that him? Is that him?" If they manage to break free from their mom, they're foraging through the forest of adult legs to get to the front of the crowd to be the first one to see Dad. Whatever they're doing, they're doing it on their tiptoes. Have you ever seen little kids run around on their tiptoes when they're excited? They look like little ballerinas. Even when they've got a clear view, they're standing on their toes. It's what kids do. They eagerly anticipate what they desire.

> *And not only the creation, but we ourselves, who have the firstfruits of the Spirit, groan inwardly as we wait eagerly for adoption as sons, the redemption of our bodies.... But if we hope for what we do not see, we wait for it with patience* (Romans 8:23, 25).

Christians would do well to develop the art of "eager anticipation" ... learning to live life on tiptoes. We especially need this skill when things are not going well, when life is hard. After all, God has given us the assignment of waiting—waiting to be delivered from the wounded world in which we live. Those who learn to wait eagerly are the ones for whom suffering produces anticipation instead of apathy or anger. Everyone has to wait, but we are given the choice as to *how* we wait.

In the language of the New Testament, at least eight Greek words were at Paul's disposal to describe waiting. He intentionally chose a word that means "to wait or expect *eagerly*." We are called to wait eagerly, not just to wait. We are called to look forward, not just to look. We are called to wait actively, not to wait passively. And most of all, we are called to wait on our tiptoes with great anticipation.

Like the newlywed whose husband cannot land soon enough, as the bride of Christ, we joyously and eagerly await the arrival of our Bridegroom—the Lord Jesus Christ. He is our hope, the reason we live life on our tiptoes. The question is: How are we waiting—as a "driver," an "associate" or an "eager"?

If you're sitting down while reading this book, stand up for a moment. Now rise up on your tiptoes. Feel good? Can you see farther? The deeper your longing for the things of God, the more of Jesus you'll see.

BRIDLED ENTHUSIASM

All parents will readily admit to the multitude of lessons they have learned from their children. But for me, one of the most spiritually helpful lessons I have learned as a parent came before my three children were born, not after.

Three times I've learned patience, twenty-seven months I've spent in the classroom of bridled enthusiasm. The lesson? It takes nine months, give or take a few days, for a baby to develop and be birthed. And no amount of impatience on my part is going to speed up that process. Tomatoes take seventy days to grow; the world takes twenty-four hours to rotate; and babies take nine months to be born. Take it or leave it, that's the way it is.

Given such an unchangeable fact, there are two ways for a husband to approach the nine months: patiently or apathetically. The apathetic husband approaches the waiting period with a wake-me-when-it's-over mentality. He's not involved; he's merely uninformed.

The patient husband, on the other hand—the one who awaits childbirth with bridled enthusiasm—is fully engaged. He decides that since he can't speed up the process, it will be more enjoyable and meaningful if he gets involved. So he's in the childbirth classes; he's running to the all-night grocery for pickles and ice cream; he's listening for the heartbeat; and he's taking up the slack with their other children. (He's up to his ears in housework and homework!) And, in spite of his enthusiasm for the process, in his daily organizer he's marking off the days one at a time. Don't get me wrong. He doesn't resent the pre-birth process. He just doesn't want it to be a *single day* longer than it needs to be ... as he waits with bridled enthusiasm.

Three times I've had to learn and relearn the lesson of how to wait. And it has been invaluable to me for this reason: Waiting for the birth of a child is a lot like waiting for the return of Christ. It's not something I have the least bit of control over. It's something that often is very trying and difficult. It's something that I would probably choose to skip if I had the option. But it's something that I am more than willing to be fully engaged in if that's what is required for me to achieve the end result. And it is something that I can choose how to respond to.

> *But if we hope for what we do not see, we wait for it with patience* (Romans 8:25).

Just like expectant fathers, you can be patient or apathetic about the life you are now living. You can slump back in your spiritual chair and tell God to wake you when it's over, feeling a little (or a lot) sorry for

yourself that the days before the big event are so difficult.
Or, you can wait patiently, with bridled enthusiasm,
for the glorious day that is coming. If you decide to
do the latter, you'll be fully engaged with God in the
experiences of your life: "Talk to me, Lord. Where's this
valley leading? What should I be learning? How are You
making me stronger? Tell me again how Your love is
making all of this work together for good. Thank You,
Lord. I'm going to hang in there with You until the end.
My hope is in You."

Tripping over the line that separates patience and apathy
is a danger during dark days. The best way to keep
your path brightly lighted is to walk in the light of God's
promises. By hoping in what you cannot see, you will
see what only hope can reveal—the path of patience, the
birthplace of perseverance.

CHECK THE BALANCE

When you sit down to pay your personal or family bills—your rent or mortgage, your utility bills, your credit card balance, your car payment—your desk is like a set of scales. On one side are the bills and on the other side is your checkbook (your laptop, really, as most of us pay everything online these days). And hopefully the scales tilt in favor of your checkbook. But if you're like most people, you pay each bill carefully. Is the amount correct? Was what I received worth the expense? Can I justify the same expense again next month?

The apostle Paul suggests that we give the same careful consideration to the experiences of our life as we do to managing our finances. You may think you do this already. But what I find as a pastor is that, in times of discouragement or trouble, most people do more worrying and speculating than they do considering. What does it mean to consider the situation you are in?

Consider is a Greek word Paul uses nineteen times in the letter to the Christians in Rome. It was used in accounting as well as the serious theological contexts in which Paul uses it in Romans: Hypocrites should consider God's judgment; God considered Abraham righteous because of his faith; God considers us righteous when we believe in Christ. "Considering" is a serious subject. So when Paul says that we are to give consideration to our experiences of suffering, he doesn't mean we are to wring our hands and speculate about our suffering. He means we are to give careful thought to the truth about our experience compared to the truth about our relationship with God.

*For I consider that the sufferings of this present time
are not worth comparing with the glory that is to be
revealed to us* (Romans 8:18).

Once again, think of it like paying your bills. If you are
going through a difficult time, Paul says to put your
experience of suffering on one side of the scales and the
glory God has promised you in heaven on the other side.
Then consider the question: Is my current experience
of suffering greater than the glory that I am going to
experience with Christ for all eternity? Sometimes it's
easy to think our suffering is greater. Time seems to
stand still when we are in pain. The hands of the clock
move as if they were mired in molasses, as if they
were cast in concrete. And if time stands still, then
this "present time" in which we suffer becomes like
eternity—we feel, we will never be freed from how we
feel. Never will we escape the suffering of this hour and
be translated into the realms of glory Paul talks about.
Easy for him to say, we think to ourselves as we consider

Paul's words. *He hasn't been where I am.*

No, he hasn't. But we haven't been where he was either. Paul wasn't theologizing when he wrote these words. He was writing as one whose entire life was a litany of suffering for the sake of the Gospel. He had been beaten, stoned, shipwrecked, slandered, had gone without food and shelter—he spent his life focused on the glory that would be revealed in and through him when he entered eternity. He viewed suffering like a window through which he saw what was soon to be his. The reasons for his suffering (to accomplish God's purposes) and the results of his suffering (conformity to the likeness of Jesus) were his constant consideration.

Have you given careful consideration to the experiences you are going through today? On the one hand is your present pain—it is real and not to be denied. But on the other hand are the permanent promises of God concerning your future with Him. If you don't see the balance tipping decidedly in the direction of glory, then you haven't yet seen your future. But you will.

Continue with me through these meditations. As you consider and compare, *your cries in hope* will start to outweigh *your cries for help*. Your tears of thankfulness for God's presence and purposes will be like an ocean as opposed to a thimbleful of your tears of doubt. When you consider today in light of tomorrow ... well, there's just no comparison.

PART TWO

God Gives Us Protection

"My sheep hear my voice, and I know them, and they follow me. I give them eternal life, and they will never perish, and no one will snatch them out of my hand."
—John 10:27–28

When we hear about evil acts and the bizarre behavior of people who lived seemingly average lives up until the time they did whatever made them newsworthy, it is hard to understand what could have motivated them to act in the way they did.

I know some people doubt the reality of Satan; they

sneer and snicker under their breath at the very idea of Satan and demonic spirits. Some think it is nothing but superstitious nonsense. And yet, more and more, people are recognizing the reality of the supernatural world. The supernatural cannot be measured by scientific discovery. But we know there is an invisible world, a powerful world that includes not only the angels of God but also the demons of hell.

The Bible gives a vivid account of demonic activity in New Testament days, and we certainly should expect that demons exist today.

I believe there are two major mistakes that people make regarding the devil and the hordes from hell that we call demons. Some underestimate the power of Satan and his influence. That is a huge mistake. We must never underestimate his power.

Others mistakenly become unduly preoccupied with demonic spirits. That must make the devil happy.

Rather than focusing on the Lord Jesus Christ and His greatness—the One who has power over all the works of the Enemy, the One who has all authority—to focus on the adversary doesn't make much sense.

As we watch our world become more and more vile and more and more wicked, it's truly frightening. The fact is that Satan *does* exist and he roams about like a prowling, roaring lion seeking whom he may devour. We must be aware of his presence but not preoccupied with him at the expense of understanding the powerful God we serve.

Our protection from the Enemy comes in the form of a person—the Person of Jesus Christ. When we come to faith in Jesus Christ, we receive a new life and a new nature. Suddenly there's a conflict. Our struggle is not with physical battles alone but with spiritual battles. Paul reminds us in Ephesians 6:12, "For we do not wrestle against flesh and blood, but against the rulers, against the authorities, against the cosmic powers over this present darkness, against the spiritual forces of evil in the heavenly places."

We need to realize our own weakness and rely upon the strength from the Lord to resist and ultimately escape the wiles of Satan.

One of my favorite personalities in the entire Bible is Joseph. He was a godly young man who had great dreams and great desires from God. Joseph's dreams led him to be sold into slavery by his own brothers and yet, even after he was taken to Egypt, Joseph knew the source of his protection and he did not give up his dreams. He did not become a spiritual casualty because he relied on the One who gave him the great dreams.

You do not need to become a spiritual casualty either. When a thought that is contrary to God's Word passes through your mind or when temptation knocks at your door, you can refuse to open the door. When you were a kid, did you ever wrestle your brother or sister to the ground and, when your sibling would struggle to get up, say, "Who's the best? Who's the coolest?" Temptation moves in like that. If we begin to entertain the idea of sin or the suggestion to disobey God, ultimately we will find ourselves in a grip that we can't escape. The devil often attempts to get us to dwell on certain sins until the desire is the biggest thing on our mind. That's why it is so important to get victory over temptation as soon as possible. We serve a powerful God. He has overcome the power of Satan, and we must learn to accept His power to protect and sustain us in this life. The Christian life does not need to be a defeated, discouraged life. We can live with confidence that the One who created us made a way for us to escape the evil of this world.

TROUBLE ON A LEASH

People who walk or jog in their neighborhoods have learned to put their faith in technology—invisible fencing. When your neighbor's dog comes racing toward you with fangs bared, you know not to worry. The wire buried around the yard sends a mild shock to the dog's collar and tells him to stop just before he has you for lunch. As many times as you've seen dogs skid to a stop within yards of where you're walking, you still wonder: *What if my neighbor forgot to turn the system on? What if it's broken? What if the dog chooses this one time to go for it and breaks through? What if, what if, what if?* You close your eyes and grit your teeth until you realize you haven't been bitten—saved again by an invisible hand.

Think of the invisible fence as an invisible leash, a rope you can't see that is played out by the owner. The dog is never out of the owner's control; your safety is always ensured. In a very elementary way, that's how you know you win in the end of this life. Regardless of how much testing God allows you to undergo, and regardless of how much confusion the devil brings across your path, this you know: Trouble is on a leash that is firmly held by God's hand. It is God who has justified you—declared you righteous. Why would He allow the one He has declared righteous to be destroyed by trouble in this world?

> *Who shall bring any charge against God's elect? It is God who justifies. Who is to condemn? Christ Jesus is the one who died—more than that, who was raised—who is at the right hand of God, who indeed is interceding for us* (Romans 8:33–34).

A man named Job in the Old Testament wished he had known that. He experienced far more trouble than you or I ever will, but he never knew while it was going on that his trouble was like a dog on a long leash. Trouble came close, to be sure. It got so close it consumed his children, his livestock and cattle, his houses—everything Job owned was consumed by Satan; everything except Job himself.

What Job didn't know, but we know (Job 1–2), was that Satan had come into the presence of God, and God pointed out His servant Job as an example of righteousness. Satan said the only reason Job was such a righteous man was that he was so prosperous. "Let me take away what he has," Satan said, "and we'll see how righteous he remains." God loosened the leash and Satan attacked, taking all of Job's property but not touching Job himself. Satan returned, saying, "Let me touch his body and you'll see him change his tune." So, God let the leash out farther: "Behold, he is in your hand, but spare his life" (Job 2:6).

Satan tormented Job by afflicting his body, but Job's life was never in danger. All the while, Job never knew that

Satan was behind his trouble; that Satan was like a dog on a leash, and that God Himself was the restrainer. He didn't know that through his suffering, he was demonstrating that God never loses that which He has saved for His own glory.

We know what was happening behind the scenes with Job, and we also have a summary of the truth we can draw from Job's story: "No temptation has overtaken you that is not common to man. God is faithful, and he will not let you be tempted beyond your ability, but with the temptation he will also provide the way of escape, that you may be able to endure it" (1 Corinthians 10:13). No one, not even Satan himself, can bring a charge against God's children—and that includes *you*. If God allows you to be tested as He did Job, remember that trouble is on a leash. An invisible fence separates you from the one who would destroy you.

So take heart as you walk through this world. Don't close your eyes and grit your teeth, hoping against hope that trouble will stop before it consumes you. Trouble is on God's leash, and you are held safely in His hand.

THE BEST PRAYER PARTNER

A pitch-black night, howling wind, horizontal rain, strange neighborhood, unfamiliar city, and your GPS is broken. You're lost. You're so lost you wouldn't know how to ask for directions even if there were anyone to ask. So you do what lots of people do—you pull over and park. You just don't know what else to do. Going forward is the same as going backward—farther into the unknown. Somebody from that city, from that neighborhood, would be nice to know at a time like this.

When you're going through difficult times in your life, that's how it can feel. You know you're lost in a strange place, and the wind and rain of trouble are trying their best to beat you into submission. They want you to just pull over to the side of the spiritual road and park. You know that's not right (you're not going to move forward by sitting still), but you're so lost you don't even know how to pray (much less feel like it) to ask God for directions. The words, "Lord, help" are in your mind, but you do not hear them leaving your lips.

> *Likewise the Spirit helps us in our weakness. For we do not know what to pray for as we ought, but the Spirit himself intercedes for us with groanings too deep for words* (Romans 8:26).

Fortunately, God has given us a Guide, someone who will help us ask for the directions we need. He knows the neighborhood, He knows how we feel, and He speaks the language we don't. If you will depend on Him, the Spirit of God will be a prayer partner to overcome four prayer problems when you are too confused to pray:

He overcomes the problem of prayerlessness. When we

have lost our way and are too discouraged to pray, we can become lethargic and apathetic about prayer. It is one of the ironies of the spiritual life that we grow less energetic about prayer at the times we need to pray most. When we're in pain, the first thing we think is that God is far away. And if He is far away, He won't hear us if we pray. Theologically, we know that reasoning has as many holes as a sieve. But we think it anyway—until the Holy Spirit arrests our thoughts, which He will. He will lead us back to prayer (Galatians 4:6).

He overcomes the problem of pain. If we do find our way to our knees, the words fail us. What should we pray for? In times of great need, it's probably true that we need to do more "listening" prayer than "talking" prayer. The Holy Spirit prays *in* and *through* us according to the will of God (Romans 8:27), giving the direction we need and don't have. He can do that because He is the Spirit of wisdom and understanding, counsel and might (Isaiah 11:2). God knows our needs when we come to Him in pain. He gives the Holy Spirit to reveal those needs, and His answers, to us in prayer.

He overcomes the problem of perspective. When we are suffering, we can have an overwhelming sense of helplessness. We're not sure who we are and we're too tired to find out. I have discovered that the Holy Spirit gives me new energy in prayer as I begin to worship. I will often listen to glorious worship music when I am struggling to find the words to pray. And I find the strength of God building in my heart as I recognize who I am in the context of who He is. But it's not music that does it; it's the Spirit of God creating praise and worship in my heart.

He overcomes the problem of powerlessness. The Holy Spirit wants you to pray. He will enter into battle on your behalf against all the distractions and confusions that rise up to keep you from praying—and make you feel powerless. When you are in the depths of despair and all hope is gone, a simple confession of your feelings will engage the armies of heaven and the Holy Spirit will empower you to pray effectively.

If you are in a dark and stormy place ... if it has been some time since you've prayed ... if you've lost your way and will ... you have a prayer partner in the Holy Spirit. But a partnership takes two. He is there, waiting.

PRAYER THAT HEALS

O ur government has an agency known as the Centers for Disease Control that has one purpose: to monitor, investigate, and seek cures for the various diseases that afflict the human race. As thorough as the agency is, there is one disease that the CDC doesn't track. It's not infectious; it doesn't respond to antibiotics; and it isn't mentioned in medical textbooks. In fact, pastors and counselors see more cases of this than doctors do. It's the disease of *introspection*.

It flares up when people suffer, when they get isolated from others due to discouraging or difficult circumstances. Almost everyone has suffered from the disease of introspection at one time or another. It's when we start focusing on ourselves, picking apart who we are and what we've done to deserve the difficult situation we are in. Our lives become like a vortex of water going down a bathtub drain, sucking everything and everyone around us into our private pain. We get so focused on ourselves that we are blind to the needs of others around us. Introspection can darken our vision and affect everyone around us.

> *Likewise the Spirit helps us in our weakness. For we do not know what to pray for as we ought, but the Spirit himself intercedes for us with groanings too deep for words. And he who searches hearts knows what is the mind of the Spirit, because the Spirit intercedes for the saints according to the will of God* (Romans 8:26–27).

I have learned to live on guard against introspection. For sure, I give my life situations sober consideration, seeking to know the will and ways of God. But I do not obsess over my pain or suffering. I do not want to get trapped in that downward spiral. Instead, I find that one of the best remedies in times of suffering is prayer—but not prayer for myself. Instead, I get my eyes off myself and ask the Holy Spirit to help me intercede for others. One of the fastest routes out of introspection is intercession for others who have needs as real as mine.

I keep a mental list of five categories of people to pray for when I myself am going through difficult times. The Holy Spirit often adjusts that list as I pray, but I am never without a place to begin. I encourage you to use this list, or create your own, as a vaccine against the disease of introspection.

Pray for those whose faith is in danger. If you know of specific people whose faith is threatened—pray for them to be strengthened, that they would survive the attacks of the Enemy or circumstances that are weakening their faith (1 Timothy 1:19).

Pray for public officials. Begin with the president of our nation and pray all the way down to the mayor of your own community. Ask God to fill public officials with righteousness and justice and wisdom to govern (1 Timothy 2:1–2).

Pray for the lost. Nothing will sort out priorities in your life like praying for the lost. Hurting for a short time cannot be compared to the fate of hurting for eternity (1 Timothy 2:3–4).

Pray for spiritual leaders. All of us have spiritual leaders at some level. Yet how often do we stop to remember that they struggle just as we do? Many pastors have no one to pastor them; they depend upon the prayers of the saints (1 Timothy 2:7–8).

Pray for the sick. Be a wounded healer by lifting up and interceding for others who are sick in soul or body. The best healers are those who have been sick themselves. If you are hurting, you know what the hurting need, so pray for them (James 5:15).

How, you may ask, am I supposed to have the spiritual strength and emotional wherewithal to pray for others when my own life is so out of sorts? You couldn't if it depended on you—but thankfully, it doesn't. The precious Holy Spirit, who lives in the heart of every believer, helps us in our weaknesses. He intercedes *for* us, but He will also intercede *through* us for others if we will make ourselves available to Him.

The disease of introspection is a one-way ticket to despair. Pray for yourself, then refocus your attention from self to others, and pray healing and helping prayers for them. I'm always amazed how quickly I am made better on the way to help someone else.

WHY DOESN'T GOD DO SOMETHING?

People in Israel were hurting. There had been no rain for several years, and they were beginning to wonder, "Why doesn't God do something?" As God's critics often suggest in difficult times, some were probably saying, "Maybe He doesn't care about our troubles. Or maybe He has no power over the rain." Every time something bad happens, people lay out the same logic: Either God cares but He lacks power, or He has power but He doesn't care. If He cares *and* has power, surely He wouldn't let us continue to suffer. Surely He would send rain.

Now Elijah was one of God's faithful prophets in the Old

Testament—and he was a character. In our modern day he might have been considered a bit irreverent—maybe even volatile. But in the rough and tumble world of ancient religion, Elijah was the guy you wanted in your corner. He knew the truth about God and the truth about idols—and he wasn't afraid to take on the false prophets of his day. Elijah knew that God was both loving and powerful, and that the drought wasn't due to any lack on God's part. (It so happened that God was withholding rain in Israel as a judgment on the wickedness of Israel's king—and as a direct answer to Elijah's prayer that He do so—but this was not due to a lack of love or ability. It was due to a bigger plan He was working out.)

To demonstrate that God's power wasn't lacking, Elijah staged a contest between himself, the prophet of God, and 450 prophets of the idol Baal. The false prophets called on Baal, and Elijah called on God. Whichever one sent fire from heaven to burn up a sacrifice would clearly be the true God. Both sides prepared sacrifices—and

Elijah soaked his with twelve jugs of water, just to make it hard to ignite. The boys of Baal went first and spent the entire day calling on the idol to send fire to consume the sacrifice. But no fire fell.

At that point, Elijah started having a little fun. He asked the Baal prophets, "Why doesn't your god do something? Maybe he's deep in thought or busy or out of town. Or maybe he's taking a nap. Maybe it will help if you shout louder!" (See 1 Kings 18:27). But their shouts went unanswered. So Elijah called on the God of Israel and asked Him to send fire from heaven so that people would know He was a powerful God who cared for them. And the fire fell. It consumed everything—including the precious water that had collected in a trench around the altar.

That day everyone in Israel who was hurting because of the drought learned two things about God: He cares and He is powerful. The fact that He was attentive to the prayers of Elijah showed that He cared. And the fact that He sent fire from heaven showed that He was powerful.

If there was no rain in Israel, it was not because God didn't care or because He was weak.

> *For the creation waits with eager longing for the revealing of the sons of God ... For we know that the whole creation has been groaning together in the pains of childbirth until now* (Romans 8:19, 22).

Have you ever wondered why God doesn't do something? Your soul may feel as parched as the floor of a Judean desert. It may have been weeks or months since you've felt the refreshment of His rains or the power of His presence. If so, I can tell you two things not to believe as you linger in this drought. It's not because God doesn't love you, nor is it because He is unable to rain His comfort and relief upon your life. Something else is at work.

All of us could look around this world at any given time and ask, "Why doesn't God do something?" Paul says the world is groaning and laboring, trying to give birth to something better. Why doesn't God just let the baby come? How much longer must our labor go on? It will go on until the perfect moment—in your life, in my life, and in the world—at which time rain will bring more glory to God than pain. Elijah was a character, but God *has* character. When His rains do come, it will be at a time and in a way that convinces you that His love and power are real.

LIFE IN A WOUNDED WORLD

The next time you are around a member of the armed forces wearing his or her dress uniform, look at the collection of ribbons worn over the heart. If you see a dark purple ribbon with white stripes binding each end, you're looking at a member of the walking wounded. That purple and white ribbon is worn by recipients of the Purple Heart, a decoration given to service members wounded in the line of duty.

Sometimes you can tell Purple Heart recipients even when they're not wearing their ribbons. They may walk with a limp, or be missing a limb, or have a noticeable scar. Even though some may have been wounded decades before you see them, they remain forever the walking wounded, because physical wounds never heal completely in this life.

You and I live in a wounded world—and we don't need a ribbon or medal to tell us so. All we have to do is look around and we can sense that something, somewhere, somehow went terribly, terribly wrong. Just as we fight back the tears when we see a wounded warrior struggling to remain hopeful, we should feel that same pain when we look at our hurting world.

> *For the creation was subjected to futility, not willingly, but because of him who subjected it, in hope that the creation itself will be set free from its bondage to corruption and obtain the freedom of the glory of the children of God* (Romans 8:20–21).

The apostle Paul tells us that the creation—the world in which we live—was subjected to futility or frustration by God Himself. You can read about this in the third chapter of Genesis. It happened when Adam and Eve chose to disobey God and go their own way. God said, "OK—so be it. But you, and the paradise I created for you to live in, will experience the consequences of your choice until I quell the rebellion in your hearts. When I do, both you and My creation will be healed forever of the wounds you have caused and received."

This is not an easy doctrine to understand, but it is an encouraging one, because Paul tells us that God infused His creation with something that would see it through the millennia of frustration it has endured. What God gave His creation was *hope*! It is almost as if this earth is a living, breathing entity. The creation exists in hope of the day when it will throw off every vestige of its sin-scarred skin and break out into a glorious freedom not known since Eden's last dawn.

And here's the good news for you: Because you are part of God's creation—distinct in His image, yet still a part—you have a hope pulsating through your veins as well. If you're a Christian, your hope is in God's Son Jesus who came to heal the world of its sin problem. But even if you haven't met Christ, you sense that God is all around you—and that knowledge gives you a hope you may never have been able to define (Romans 1:19–20). Hope is God's gift to His creation—which means you.

Soldiers in the killing fields of war don't always know whether they will survive their wounds. But you can know. When your hope is directed toward the promises of God in Christ, you can know that you will walk again—both now and forever. Although God may not erase your scars until a day in the future, you can know—you can live in hopeful anticipation—that day is coming.

In The Message version of the Bible, Paul's words are transcribed this way:

> *The created world itself can hardly wait for what's coming next. Everything in creation is being more or*

less held back. God reins it in until both creation and all the creatures are ready and can be released at the same moment into the glorious times ahead. Meanwhile, the joyful anticipation deepens (Romans 8:19–21).

Isn't that good? *The joyful anticipation deepens!* I pray that you are living in joyful anticipation—living in hope— today. I pray that when others see you, though they may see the wounds of this life, they will see something more, even from a distance. They may not see a Purple Heart on your chest, but I pray that they will see a Hopeful Heart *within* it.

PART THREE

God Gives Us Purpose

Be watchful, stand firm in the faith, act like men, be strong. —1 Corinthians 16:13

The familiar Bible story of David and Goliath is taught to children and preached from pulpits on a regular basis. The young shepherd boy David is applauded for his courage. The story is more than a children's story, and it's more than a story of a great fight between a young shepherd boy and the giant Goliath.

It's the story about a clash between good and evil. It's a powerful picture of our own battles and the promise of victory that we have in Jesus Christ.

I want you to think about why David was so courageous. Remember, the children of Israel were encamped on the hillside of the side of the Valley of Elah. We can go today to the Valley of Elah and stand in the very place where the battle took place. On one side of the hill were the children of Israel, and in the camp beneath were the Philistines—the cruel, ironclad Philistines—pagans who did not know the one true God of Israel.

A giant represented the Philistines. We know him as Goliath. He was a powerful man. According to Scripture, he stood between nine and ten feet tall. With his helmet on, he would have reached almost eleven or twelve feet—a massive creature. He would have been a top draft pick in the NBA!

Goliath was powerful and strong. He probably weighed around four hundred pounds because we know the armor he wore weighed between 150 and 200 pounds.

He carried a spear like a utility pole, and the head of the spear weighed twenty or twenty-five pounds. He was the Incredible Hulk and Darth Vader wrapped up into one.

The giant man had more protection. He had a shield bearer, the Scripture says, someone who walked in front of him and carried a shield that was as big as a man to protect Goliath against any errant arrow that might be flying his way. I've often thought about that guy carrying the shield for Goliath. I envision him strutting in front of this massive man saying, "Yeah, he's THE man! He's THE man!"

Day after day this intimidating presence moved closer and closer to the encampment of Israel defying the armies of God and God Almighty Himself, shouting and cursing obscenities.

We all face giants in our lives. Maybe you face giants of envy or jealousy or temptation or moral challenges. Giants of worry and fear grip the hearts of many.

The scene changes. God's champion, David the

shepherd boy, enters. He'd been anointed to be the king of Israel, but he was still a shepherd at this point. He'd not yet ascended to the throne. He was probably just a typical teenager, nothing special in appearance.

But there was something about this young man that was different. He had a heart for God. His very name, David, means *the apple of God's eye.* Scripture reminds us that God does not measure strength and power by outward appearance, but He looks at the heart. If you want to measure an individual, don't measure the head; put the tape around the heart.

I want to show you how we, like David, can win our battles and experience success in God's eyes. First Samuel 17:29–30 (NKJV) holds the key: "And David said, 'What have I done now? *Is there* not a cause?' Then he turned from him toward another and said the same thing."

"*Is there* not a cause?" If you're going to survive or thrive in life, you must have a cause. David's cause was the honor and the glory of God. He would not let a foul Philistine defy the armies of God and blaspheme the name of the Lord.

The Israelites were shaking in their sandals on the side of the hill. They had forgotten who they were and why they were there. Little minds have a desire to win, but great minds have the determination and courage to win because they have a cause. Do you know your cause in life? It's our purpose that keeps us going against all odds.

I read an acrostic on "purpose." It is purpose that separates the ordinary from the extraordinary in life:

Pray
Unite
Risk
Plan
Observe
Sacrifice
Expect

If you have a cause and your cause is for the glory of God, it's going to make a difference in your life, a huge difference. It is not intellect alone that God uses, or education or good looks or popularity or wealth, but it's great hearts—men and women who are dominated by a passionate cause. David charged the giant and changed the world because he loved God more than life.

Now, more than ever, we are facing a similar conflict in our world—a clash of cultures, a clash between good and evil, a clash between God and antichrists. The war is for the soul of our nation and the souls of the world.

Some would suggest that we retreat to our churches and forget about saving the lost, but this is not a time for Christians to retreat from the battle. It's time to get into the battle and stay in the battle against evil and the forces of hell.

There comes a time in our lives when we must say, "Enough! I'll not allow you to blaspheme the name of my God anymore." When we stand for truth and righteousness, our cause defines our purpose. *"For the eyes of the LORD run to and fro throughout the whole earth, to show Himself strong on behalf of those whose heart is loyal to Him"* (2 Chronicles 16:9).

There is a major difference between positive thinking and positive faith. Positive thinking is good as far as it takes you, but positive faith says, "I can do all things through Christ who strengthens me."

The battle is the Lord's. Our purpose is to commit our lives to Him. Jesus said if your faith is even the size of a mustard seed, you'll say to the mountain (or giant), "be removed," and it shall be cast into the sea. He was reassuring us that the smallest amount of faith is bigger than our biggest obstacle.

TAKE CARE OF YOUR CONSCIENCE

The story goes that a few weeks after attending church and hearing a sermon on "secret sins," a man wrote the following letter to the Internal Revenue Service: "Dear Sirs, I have been unable to sleep at night knowing that I have cheated on my income tax. I understated my taxable income last year by a significant amount and my conscience has bothered me ever since. Enclosed please find a check for $150. If I find that I still can't sleep, I will send the rest."

Pastors, counselors, and psychiatrists see all too often the debilitating effects of guilt. Guilt leads to stress and anxiety, which lead to conflicts in every area of life—not to mention long-term physical problems as well. Tranquilizing medicines have become drugs of choice in America for a culture intent on numbing the pain in their souls and self-medicating to bury their sins and the burdens of life.

The good news is that consciences can be made clean by accepting the gift of forgiveness God offers to every person. Sin is not swept under the rug or winked at. Instead, our sins were paid for by a sinless sacrifice, God's own Son. Until a person's sin has been forgiven by God, the conscience remains shackled by guilt. And that guilt is kept at the forefront of the mind by the efforts of one known as the Accuser, Satan himself. If a person chooses to retain his sins, he becomes fair game for the Accuser who condemns sinners before the throne of God (Revelation 12:10). Often I have seen lives turned around, depression relieved, relationships restored, and hope imparted simply by confessing hidden and secret sin. A clear conscience, gained through faith in Christ, is a prerequisite for hopeful and healthy living. "Who shall bring any charge against God's elect? It is God who justifies" (Romans 8:33).

But something else can happen in the realm of the conscience—and we are seeing this more and more as horrendous sin seems more widespread than ever. Many people are coming to Christ with consciences drastically seared by the memories of serious sin. For instance, nearly 60 million babies have been aborted in America since 1973. Adultery now seems to be an accepted part of a culture that seeks pleasure at any cost. And like everything else, marriage vows are seemingly disposable, tossed away as easily as empty water bottles. Our prisons are filled with sexual predators and murderers, ruthless criminals of every sort who have no respect for life.

But then something glorious happens. These individuals find Jesus Christ and discover the cleansing power of His blood. All their sins, big or small, are washed away and they are made clean (1 Corinthians 6:9–11).

The catharsis of finding freedom from the guilt of sin is overwhelming. Darkness is dispelled, clouds are blown away, spirits are lifted, hope for the future is restored. Unless ... unless they fail to take care of their consciences.

First, they may allow the Accuser to come in and steal their joy, their freedom and their hope by reminding them of just what vile sinners they were, and still are. The Accuser likes nothing better than to plant seeds of doubt in the mind of a forgiven sinner: "You just think you're forgiven. Do you really think God could forgive somebody like you?" Joy and hope begin to disappear like the retreating tide on a beach—too little to notice at once, but too much not to notice over time.

Second, they may fail to keep their consciences clean. Sometimes it's easy to think that since God has forgiven me of huge sins in the past, gossiping at church is not that big of a deal. Sin is sin, isn't it? It doesn't matter whether an expensive watch stops because of a tiny piece of sand or because it was smashed by a hammer. Either one will shut it down.

If you've experienced the release from sin that Jesus provides, maintain your joy by taking care of your conscience. Never have hope and joy been more freely available to those who will take God at His Word: "Your sins are forgiven you."

A REALITY CHECK

The dictionary defines *paranoia* as "a psychotic disorder characterized by delusions of persecution or grandeur." True paranoia can cause people to pull down the shades on the windows of their lives for fear that "someone is out to get me." The idea that it is "me against the world" can shackle the person for whom such delusions represent reality.

On the other hand, understanding who is out to get you is necessary if you are a believer. In other words, if you sometimes experience a general sense of weariness from just being alive, it could be because there really is something out to get you. And that something is the world. Christians often forget that living in this world is like spending your life swimming against the current. It never lets up. There is never a moment when you can just relax and float downstream. If you do, you start drifting in the direction of the world and away from the kingdom of God.

> *Who is to condemn? Christ Jesus is the one who died—more than that, who was raised—who is at the right hand of God, who indeed is interceding for us.* (Romans 8:34).

Before you became a Christian, living in this world was easy. You didn't know it, but you were part of the world, going with the flow. But when you met Jesus, you were called to go in a different direction. I have heard young believers ask, "Why is life so much harder now that I'm a Christian? I thought coming to Jesus was supposed to make things easier!" Well, it does and it doesn't. Coming to Jesus solves some problems such as being released from the condemnation of sin. But coming to

Jesus creates other problems—like making you odd man out in worldly terms. The way of life that was once your comfort zone is no longer. But you still have to live and work in it every day. You now have to be *in* the world without being *of* the world. And that can take its toll.

The J.B. Phillips paraphrase of Romans 12:2 says, "Don't let the world around you squeeze you into its own mould."[1] Think about those words. First, it implies that the world is alive and well with an agenda of its own. Do you ever think of the world as "alive"? If you don't, you should. It is alive because "the whole world lies in the power of the evil one" (1 John 5:19). The heartbeat of this world (in its fallen state as Paul discusses in Romans 8) is the heartbeat of Satan himself. That is a strong statement, but one you need to come to grips with to understand how easy it is to grow weary in this world.

Second, it implies that there is constant pressure being exerted on you. The world is trying to reshape

---

1 The New Testament in Modern English, translated by J. B. Phillips (New York: Macmillan, 1958).

you. And that's got to hurt! Think about trying
to squeeze one more item into an already-stuffed
suitcase when packing for a trip. You poke, you cram,
you sit on the lid to try to make it close. Squeezing
anything into an unnatural shape calls for pressure.
And when the world is constantly squeezing you into
its mold, then your heart, soul, mind, and body are
going to feel the pressure.

One final thought (and this is not paranoia, it's the
truth): There is someone who doesn't want you to have a
moment of rest. Colossians 1:13 says, "He has delivered
us from the domain of darkness and transferred us to
the kingdom of his beloved Son." If you are a Christian,
you were rescued from someone who had you ... and that
someone employs continual schemes by which to make
your life miserable (Ephesians 6:11).

You will grow weary in this world. But Jesus Christ,
who loves you and redeemed you, is at the right hand
of God making intercession for you so that you will not

fail. And *"He who is in you is greater than he who is in the world"* (1 John 4:4).

FATE OR FAITH?

In 1956, the noted filmmaker Alfred Hitchcock produced a second version of his 1934 movie, *The Man Who Knew Too Much.* This classic, updated version of the film starred James Stewart and Doris Day as an American couple vacationing in Morocco with their son. They accidentally become aware of an assassination plot, and their son is kidnaped by the assassins to ensure their silence. The movie proceeds from that point in typical Hitchcock fashion—ordinary people being swept up in chaotic, frightening circumstances totally beyond their control. *The Man Who Knew Too Much* won an Oscar for best song, "Que Sera, Sera." The song is catchy and creative, but its chorus offers little hope for folks desperately trying to escape the tangled web presented in the movie: "Que sera, sera. Whatever will be, will be; the future's not ours to see. Que sera, sera."

Whatever will be, will be? Is that the best life has to offer? For many people, I'm afraid it is. How many times do we hear folks use the expression, "Whatever." That's just a shortened version of "Que sera, sera." I'm sorry to say that I even hear Christians summarizing their approach to a given situation under the "Whatever" label. When Christians exchange their faith for fatalism, we've got problems. I know people, especially young people, who use that phrase aren't doing so as an expression of a well-thought-out philosophical worldview. But our words reflect what we believe. "Out of the abundance of the heart the mouth speaks" (Matthew 12:34).

Let me ask you—do you ever throw up your hands or roll your eyes and conclude, "Whatever" about your life? Most of us have never found ourselves in the life threatening, chaotic situation conceived by Mr.

Hitchcock. And yet, as they say, life imitates art all too often. Life does get chaotic. It can seem out of control. And if your physical life isn't being threatened, you might feel as though your spiritual, emotional, and mental lives are. So how is a believer's faith supposed to help when it looks as though fate has taken over? How do we respond when life seems as controllable as an avalanche in the Swiss Alps—with you being swept up, carried along, and buried under a pile at the bottom?

Faith is when you believe the Bible and act accordingly: "And we know that for those who love God all things work together for good, for those who are called according to his purpose." The person of faith believes that all things—even the kidnapping of a child as happened in the movie—work together for good to those who love God. As I write these words, I think of Pastor Saeed Abedini, held in an Iranian prison since 2012 for "undermining national security." His crime—helping to start Christian house churches a decade earlier. His young children in Idaho have been without their father for almost half their lives, and his wife, Naghmeh, pleads for his release. Despite demands from our country that he be freed, he remains in prison in life-threatening conditions.

But his family hasn't lost hope. If the Abedinis—a family whose life has been torn apart for more than three years—can have faith that all things work together for good, I believe I can too.

And I believe you can as well. But there is a condition. The apostle Paul doesn't apply this promise to every person on earth. He says it is for those "who love God … who are called according to His purpose." Those who have demonstrated their love for God, proven they are the called by believing in Christ, are the ones for whom fate is replaced by faith.

Are you one of those? If so, then begin walking today by faith, not by fate. If "Que Sera, Sera" is your motto, then step one is to believe in Christ. It's the only way to be certain that all things are working together for good.

> *"And we know that all things work together for good to those who love God, to those who are the called according to His purpose"* (Romans 8:28).

THE PURPOSE OF IT ALL

O n a day when you're wondering, "What's it all about?" I encourage you to turn away from the secular worldview of our day. Your cloudy day will grow darker if you don't. Why? Well, see how encouraging this sounds:

Around three or four billion years ago, a speck of life accidentally appeared somewhere on this planet. It probably arose when a bolt of lightning struck a pool of muck and something happened that caused something to come alive. Over the following millions and millions of years, that speck of life survived, prospered, duplicated itself, became a cell, became an organism, became a creature, and became a human being.

There you have it. That's how you happen to be here today, according to the priests of No-Purpose Religion. As one adherent of this random origin of life theory says, "Man is the result of a purposeless and natural process that did not have him in mind. He was not planned. He is a state of matter, a form of life, a sort of animal...." To put it bluntly, you're an accident.

Other scientists and philosophers who hold to the evolutionary worldview have been equally encouraging about the purpose of our lives. One said man is merely a "hairless ape." Another said we are "a fungus on the surface of one of the minor planets." Another says humanity is "a rope stretched over an abyss." Hmmmm. I don't know about you, but I'm feeling better about my life already!

Is it any wonder that so many people today live without a purpose in life? We are in the midst of reaping the seeds of secular humanism that were sown in America in the twentieth century. *The Humanist Manifesto I*, published in 1933, was signed by thirty-four American scholars and scientists, including John Dewey, the father of the American public school system. The purpose of the manifesto was to promote a religion of humanism that had no god but man. By the early 1960s, prayer and Bible reading were removed from our schools and the government sanctioned a "wholly secular" approach to teaching children. That approach can have no other outcome except to produce young people who believe— unless they've been taught differently at home or in church—that there is little purpose in life. "Life is an accident" is the best the secularists have to offer.

As pastor of a large church that ministers to thousands of people weekly, I can tell you that even many Christians succumb to the pervasive influences of humanism in our culture. Because it is the prevailing view of education and the media, it might as well be in the air we breathe and the water we drink. Many Christians struggle to understand the purpose of life in general and their purpose in particular.

Everyone needs clarification, direction, counseling, and advice about one's purpose in life. But that's different from the creeping sense that life is a series of mechanical motions we go through today simply because we did them yesterday. That kind of dead-end mentality about life can be debilitating at best and destructive at worst. It needs to be confronted with the truth. If you are a Christian, there is a crystal-clear purpose for your life: You have been called by God to be conformed to the likeness of Jesus Christ and to take up an eternal place in God's family forever.

> *For those whom he foreknew he also predestined to be conformed to the image of his Son, in order that he might be the firstborn among many brothers* (Romans 8:29).

Remember what we've learned about this wounded

world we live in—we're just a-passin' through, as the old gospel song says. Our purpose is to follow the call of God through this world to the eternal home He is preparing—the new heavens and new earth—where we will abide with Him forever. That doesn't mean this life doesn't matter. It means the present always gains its clearest perspective when seen in light of the future.

There are no accidents with God. You are not the current manifestation of something that crawled out of a primordial puddle a few billion years ago. Rather, you are a person purposefully created by God who has numbered all your days (Psalm 139:13–16). Your purpose in this life is to know Him now and prepare to enjoy Him forever.

PAIN AND GAIN

We humans are like sponges, aren't we? Plop us down in a bowl of contemporary culture, and in a matter of years we've soaked it all up without even realizing it. Then life comes along and squeezes us hard, and out come the beliefs we've absorbed. Take suffering, for instance.

Who is not familiar with the saying, "No Pain, No Gain!"? Parents tell it to their finger-sore children to get them to practice their piano scales. Coaches scream it at their noodle-legged players when making them run sprint intervals on the track. And bosses preach it to their sleep-starved employees to get them to pull yet another all-nighter before the initial public offering of their company's stock. No Pain, No Gain. To be technical, we could say it's a two-phase linear process. That is, first comes the pain, then comes the gain: no piano solos without practicing scales, no Super Bowl rings without running sprints, no overnight wealth without all-night work.

Before we get too critical of this way of thinking, let's agree that life does require hard work—and hard work is generally painful in some way or the other. But here's the dangerous part of the No Pain, No Gain mentality from a Christian perspective: It implies that first you have to suffer the pain before God will give you the gain. And we equate the "pain" God requires of us with the times of trouble and suffering we all experience. Therefore, without even knowing it, when we find ourselves in the midst of difficult times, it's easy to lapse into a dues-paying mentality: "This is just the price of my admission to heaven." Or, "This is just my cross to bear." Or, "Things could always be worse."

If that's how you think when trouble comes, you can bet your last damp tissue that you've bought into the culture's flawed mentality. Hear me when I say, your pain is not sent to you by God in exchange for your entrance into heaven. Nor is your pain sent to you by God to toughen you up, to make a spiritual Olympian out of you. If it were, at some point all of us would say (as many musicians, athletes, and entrepreneurs do), "This isn't worth it. I quit." It's hard enough to stay focused for twelve months on a Super Bowl ring you can see and touch and feel. In the Christian life you have to stay focused for a lifetime on an invisible eternity. We need more than No Pain, No Gain to make it. Sadly, some Christians do throw in the towel in the midst of suffering. But I don't want you to be one of them.

Here's the truth about pain and gain. Your gain is a *gift* from God: "You have been saved through faith ... it is the gift of God, not of works ..." (Ephesians 2:8–9). Your pain cannot earn what you've already been given as a gift. Your pain is a result of living in a fallen, pain-filled world. Living in this world is like a fish living in the ocean. A fish doesn't get wet; it *is* wet! Wet is all it has ever known. In the same way, life in this world is painful. There are tears when we're born and tears when we die. Ever since man first disobeyed God, he has been living by the sweat of his brow—trying to keep the briars from overtaking the berries (Genesis 3:17–19).

> *For I consider that the sufferings of this present time are not worth comparing with the glory that is to be revealed to us* (Romans 8:18).

So, instead of pain being the prerequisite for gain, think of it this way: Life has both pain *and* gain. If you are a Christian, Paul says that unbelievable glory awaits you, glory that is a pure gift from God. And because God is your Father who will not allow you to miss out on the gift He has given you, He has promised to escort you through the painful parts of this life. He guarantees your gain while accompanying you in your pain. That's truth worth soaking up, isn't it?

PART FOUR

God Gives Us Power

Now to him who is able to do far more abundantly than all that we ask or think, according to the power at work within us, to him be glory in the church and in Christ Jesus throughout all generations, forever and ever. Amen. —Ephesians 3:20–21

A confident life ... if there's anything we need in these uncertain and insecure times, it is the security and confidence that can come only from knowing Jesus Christ. Words such as *assurance* and *security* and *confidence* ought to be a part of the daily vocabulary of the child of God. We can move forward into the future with confidence, not in ourselves, but in the God we serve and the Gospel that we have received.

In 2 Timothy 1:12 (NKJV), Paul gives us a statement that we all need to memorize: "For this reason I also suffer these things; nevertheless I am not ashamed, for I know whom I have believed and am persuaded that He is able to keep what I have committed to Him until that Day."

You may say, "Well, that's easy enough for Paul to say. After all, Paul was a supernatural, powerful Christian. Paul was a power preacher. He was a missionary. He was an apostle, for goodness sake." However, these words were not written from a pulpit, but from a prison. Paul was facing incredible obstacles in his own life, yet he said, "I know whom I have believed." There is incredible confidence in the words he spoke.

The confidence Paul expressed was not coming from a man who was just naturally optimistic. As a matter of fact, as I review the life of Paul from the Scriptures, I would say that Paul was not naturally optimistic. I would say Paul was supernaturally optimistic, for naturally in the human sense his temperament was rather melancholy at times. He faced fear, he faced problems, and Paul had a tendency to become very serious and very stoic. Yet he had experienced the reality of a new life in Christ, and that new life was filled with purpose and confidence. When he raises that conjunction "nevertheless ..." it's a protest, a powerful persuasion in which he rises above and overcomes in life.

There ought to be a "nevertheless" written across every believer's life—not necessarily because every believer is an extrovert and naturally optimistic. You may be introverted, and you may tend to be pessimistic. So we're not *born optimists*, we are *born-again optimists*. We are optimists because we know our purpose and we know what Paul knew when he said, "I know whom I have believed." In these uncertain times we need to be certain of the purpose of the One who called us. And because of what the apostle knew and because of what we know, we can live a life with power and confidence.

Now, when you start living passionately for the Lord Jesus Christ, you're going to get the devil's attention, and you're going to have some problems. I believe one of the devil's most powerful tools is discouragement. But remember, you have a divine power and you must persevere. Determination in the Christian life turns the *ordinary* into the *extraordinary*.

Great men and women are spiritually marked by perseverance. You measure a man not by what it takes to start him, but what it takes to stop him. You couldn't stop the apostle Paul no matter what. He said, "Hey, heads, I win ... tails, I win." And Paul provides us with Scripture for life in Philippians 1:21: "For to me to live is Christ, and to die is gain." He was assaulted with temptations to give up and to quit, but he would not quit! Why? Because he said, "I know whom I have believed."

You don't determine greatness by talent or wealth
or education or personality but by the work of God's
grace in a man's or woman's heart. Living a life with
power; persevering all the way to the end; relying on the
Spirit—not on the human spirit but upon the Spirit of
God—that's what Paul is saying to us.

Living a life with power is truly defined when we realize
where we are going. We are on our way to heaven. We're
destined for glory. We're not afraid. No distraction, no
disease, no death can separate us from the love of God
that is in Christ Jesus.

When tragedy strikes our families or our country, we hear
more talk about heaven, and with every friend or loved
one who dies, heaven becomes just a little dearer. Earth is
just the warm-up. What we are going through now is just
the preparation. Heaven is what life is all about.

Set your affections above and not on this earth. Find
the real purpose for which God created you. Then when

you look into the future, there is no fear, there is no pain, there is no loneliness, there is no need, there is no problem. Whatever it is that we may face, nothing can shake our confidence or deter our purpose because God watches over us, His grace works within us, and heaven awaits us.

SATISFACTION GUARANTEED

I am not sure how it started or where it will end, but I'm all for it—this emphasis on customer satisfaction in the marketplace. It's not that it didn't exist before, but it has taken on a new tone over the years.

For instance, I can remember when there was no such thing as price-matching ("If you can find this product at a cheaper price, we will match it and take another 10 percent off!"). And you would never expect a store to honor another store's coupons, or to see companies battling each other in cyber sales wars. But that happens all the time in today's market. And what about returns? People don't hesitate today to return anything for any reason. One upscale department store chain that is well known for customer satisfaction allowed a man to return a set of tires he swore he bought at their store in another city—even though they don't carry tires in any of their stores.

Maybe the biggest advance in customer satisfaction has been in the simplifying of product guarantees. It used to be that guarantees were written by lawyers for lawyers and read only by people who owned magnifying glasses. Now they usually read like this: "If anything you purchase from us is found to be unsatisfactory, we will make it right in a way that satisfies you. No questions asked. Guaranteed." When I see guarantees like that, it makes me think the store's lawyers have been reading Romans 8:29–30.

If you will allow me a crude comparison, we tend to equate the spiritual life with a shopping experience. At the mall, we exchange our money for something we hope will add some benefit or satisfaction to our life, and when it doesn't we reach for the guarantee (if we didn't throw it out in the trash). If it's understandable, we rejoice and take the appropriate steps to resolve our disappointment. In a similar way, in the spiritual life, we exchange not money but our whole life for a promise from God that we will be reconciled to Him" and "have life and have it abundantly" (John 10:10). But then, the inevitable disappointments in life come. The product—our spiritual life—doesn't meet our expectations. Our consumer mentality makes us want to approach God and say "What gives, Lord? I didn't expect this product to act like this." If you recall, a man named Job in the Old Testament asked God those very sorts of questions when his life fell apart.

May I tell you up front, God doesn't mind your asking Him questions about your life. He created you and gave you your new life in Christ as a gift, and He wants you to be fully satisfied with it. But here's the catch that separates shopping from the spiritual life: To be satisfied with your life, you have to be satisfied with God. He has written a guarantee for your life that is in His terms, not yours. But once you understand it, I think you'll be able to relax and be satisfied with this product we call "life."

God's guarantee has five parts. Four of them have taken place in the past, and one is yet to be completed (in a manner of speaking). Here's what has already happened to you as a believer in Christ: *God foreknew you* (that means He chose you to be His before you ever existed); *He predestined you* (He sealed your ultimate eternal destiny); *He called you* (He opened your spiritual eyes and ears to hear and respond to the Gospel); and *He justified you* (He declared you free from all your sins).

The fifth part of the guarantee is the best of all: *He glorified you.* Now we know that occurs in the future—that is Paul's whole point in Romans 8. But grammatically, Paul uses the same past tense language to describe your future as he does your past. That is, your future glory is as good as done. In modern customer satisfaction terms, it's as if God is saying, *"Before you get home and try this product, your ultimate, eternal glory is personally guaranteed by Me."*

How is your life working today, this week, this month? If it has been rough, don't despair. You have His word that your glory is guaranteed.

IT IS FINISHED

When Adolf Hitler was in the early stages of attempting to consolidate all of Europe under the flag of Nazism, one world leader saw the future more clearly than any other. England's Winston Churchill was a lone voice, warning others not to come to terms with Hitler but to resist him. He turned out to be right. Churchill said, "I have read so far back in history that I'm able to see further ahead in the future."

Reading back in history often yields insights that help us overcome our spiritual challenges. If we turn back just a few pages in our modern history books, we'll discover why no Christian should ever fear the emotional, financial, spiritual, even the physical assaults that come against us in our lives. And interestingly, Mr. Churchill is at the center of the story again.

England was in Hitler's sights. He knew that to capture all of Europe, he must cross the English Channel and conquer England—and Churchill knew that was his plan. Churchill also knew England could not stop Hitler alone, and he turned to America for help. America was reluctant to get involved in the struggle for Europe. We had already entered into a massive conflict against Japan in the South Pacific in 1941. But after many months of delay—during which time England was greatly damaged by Nazi planes and rockets—President Franklin D. Roosevelt committed the United States to join the Allied nations (Russia, France, Great Britain) against the Axis nations (Germany, Italy, Japan).

From the hindsight of history, the day the United States joined the Allies, World War II was essentially over. Winston Churchill could easily have sunk down into a chair, dosed his eyes, and whispered, "If America be for us, who can stand against us?" Of course, no one knew that at the time. No one knew whether America and the Allies could defeat the massive German armies that were overrunning Europe. But on D-Day, when the Allies stormed ashore on the beaches of France on June 6, 1944, Germany's fate was sealed. There was still much blood to be spilled, many battles to be fought, and great heartache to be felt over lives lost. But by August of 1945, World War II was over.

It took more than a year for the Allies to experience what was established in fact many months before. It always takes time for the truth to work itself out in life. And in the interim, life is lived on the basis of promise and commitment. The day Churchill learned that America was joining the fight, his challenge was to hang on until victory became reality. And such is the challenge in the spiritual life.

What then shall we say to these things? If God is for us, who can be against us? He who did not spare his own Son but gave him up for us all, how will he not also with him graciously give us all things? (Romans 8:31–32).

The equivalent of D-Day in the world of spiritual warfare was a day in the spring of A.D. 33. On that day, God gave His own Son to be nailed to a cross, an act that cancelled out all the accusations of sin our Enemy could bring against us (Colossians 2:13–16). Less than seventy-two hours later, God defeated the last enemy, death, by raising that same Son from the dead. By those two acts, God destroyed all the work of our archenemy, Satan (1 John 3:8). When Jesus said, "It is finished"—it *was* finished.

Just as in the real world, in the spiritual world the battle continues even after the victory is sealed. If the truth you have just read is new to you, or if you have failed to depend on it of late, now is the time for you to sink down in your chair, close your eyes, and

whisper, "If God is for me, who can be against me?
If He has given His own Son for me, will He not also
give me strength, hope, daily bread, money to pay
my bills, love for my spouse and children, strength to
resist sin ... everything I need?" The answer is, "Yes,
He will." We are living in the days between the Cross
and the crown. There will be hardships to endure but
no ultimate defeats. The victory is yours.

YOUR DESTINY

Survey a roomful of scholars and you'll probably get a roomful of answers to this question: "At what point in history did the destiny of the world hang in the balance?" I'm not a scholar, but I am going to be so bold as to profess that I know the answer. I know the day when the destiny of the entire human race was in one man's hands.

Before you say—"What's the point? I've got bills to pay, arguing kids to separate, carpool to drive, and a job to find"—hear me out. You may not think the destiny of the human race is on your plate today, but I know something that is: the destiny of your life and the lives of those you love. Think about it. Whatever action or decision saved the human race might be able to save you from the next crisis that confronts your life (or the one you're in today). Enough theorizing—here's the story.

"Then Jesus was led up by the Spirit into the wilderness to be tempted by the devil" (Matthew 4:1). You might think that something as weighty as I've mentioned would have been played out in a throne room or a gilded court or at least on a battlefield stained with the blood of the good and evil. That's how Hollywood might portray it, but it was nowhere near that predictable. In fact, it took place in the Judean desert, observed only by snakes and scorpions, beetles and bandits. In that place, Satan approached the Son of God to see if He would swap His birthright for a full stomach, a magician's mantle, and an earthly crown.

You see, Satan had been successful in tempting the first-created child of God, Adam, in the Garden of Eden. In fact, all the trouble Paul refers to in Romans 8 had its beginning when Adam and Eve yielded to the lust of the flesh, the lust of the eyes, and the boastful pride of life Satan laid before them. So when Jesus came as the last Adam to win back what the first Adam lost, we might have expected Satan to cast his shadow across the scene.

Three times Satan tempted Jesus. Jesus had been without food for forty days, so Satan encouraged Him to break His fast and turn a stone into bread. Next, Satan tempted Jesus to win the acclaim of the crowds by performing a miracle at the temple. Finally, he tempted the Son to give up the crown that would be won at the Cross for one that was available by crossing over: Give up the kingdom of God to rule the kingdoms of this world.

Your destiny and mine were hanging in the balance that day. If Jesus had given in to the tempter's offer, we would forever live outside the gates of Eden where our forebears Adam and Eve found themselves. But if Jesus stood fast, He would win back power over sin and temptation and make His way to the Cross where an eternal crown and kingdom would be His—and ours. Three times Jesus denied the temptations of the devil. He refused the lusts of the flesh, the lust of the eyes, and boastful pride of life by obeying the Word of God.

Just as the devil approached Jesus, "principalities and powers" often come to us in the deserts of our life. We are starving for hope and deliverance, lusting after what we can see but can't have, and longing for a prideful position with resources to insulate us from the troubles of this world. The human race doesn't depend on our choices, but our lives and usefulness do. Paul tells us that nothing—not even the devil and his principalities and powers—can separate us from the protective love God has for us. No crisis you are in is beyond God and His resources if you will remain faithful to God and His Word. The path out of the desert back to the green valley is always paved with truth. If you know and obey the truth, it will set you free from any temptation, and it will defeat any scheme of the devil. Indeed, it will save your life.

LOVE THAT WILL NOT FAIL

We have sung "Jesus Loves Me" since we were children. Those words roll off our tongues with such familiarity that we are almost insulated against their power and meaning. Really—how does the fact that Jesus loves me affect my discouragement, my despair, or the days when my desire to be faithful seems like too little, too late?

Who shall separate us from the love of Christ? Shall tribulation, or distress, or persecution, or famine, or nakedness, or danger, or sword? As it is written, "For your sake we are being killed all the day long; we are regarded as sheep to be slaughtered." No, in all these things we are more than conquerors through him who loved us (Romans 8:35–37).

We have to remember that when Paul wrote those words to the Christians in Rome, he was writing from his own personal experiences with the love of Jesus Christ. Because that love has not changed and will not change, our experiences may be different from those of the Christians in Rome, but the One who made them "more than conquerors" is still the One we need to call on today.

What was Paul's experience with "Jesus loves me"? He lists different categories he had been through as a Christian: tribulation, distress, persecution, famine, nakedness, peril, and sword. When Paul wrote this letter, he had not yet been through some of the greatest difficulties that awaited him near the end of his missionary career in Jerusalem and Rome. So what he mentions here is just the half of it (a fuller picture is in 2 Corinthians 6 and 11). But the troubles he had been through by this point in his life had convinced him of this: They did not mean that Jesus didn't love him.

When Paul was in trouble or distress, *Jesus was loving him*. When he was being persecuted for being a Christian, *Jesus was loving him*. When he had no food or clothing, *Jesus was loving him*. When he found himself staring at the sharp end of a sword, *Jesus was loving him*. In fact, Paul's willingness to continue to endure life's hardships without giving up was evidence that Jesus loved him. How is that true, you may wonder. Because Paul knew a cardinal truth that the apostle John later wrote down: "We love because he first loved us" (1 John 4:19).

Make sure you understand this dynamic. The Bible tells us clearly that our love for Christ—our willingness not to give up, to maintain hope, to obey Him even when things are difficult—does not arise naturally within us. We love Him only because He first loved us. Our love for Him, our willingness to persevere all the way to the end, is evidence that Jesus loves us. The question is not, "Can difficult times make me stop loving Christ?" The question is, "Do difficult times mean Christ has stopped loving me?" And the answer is a resounding, eternal, NO! Nothing can make Christ stop loving us.

When was the last time you had no food or clothes, were beaten for being a Christian, or were threatened with a gun or sword for your faith? For some Christians in the world today, the words of Paul have direct meaning because they are experiencing these hardships. But most of us are not. So how do we apply his words? Perhaps this way: "Who or what then can separate us from the love of Christ? Can a spouse who is unfaithful? Can my own lack of faithfulness? Can a rebellious child? Can a boss who fires me, a friend who betrays me, a disease that disables me, a future that discourages me? No, in spite of all these things I will win in the end because Jesus loves me!"

Overcoming life's challenges does not ultimately depend

on your strength, will or grit. It depends on whether or not Jesus loves you. And because He does, and always will, you will overcome—and win in the end.

ARE YOU CONVINCED?

Most often, when we see people walking through difficult circumstances in life, we say they are people of great faith. "Keep the faith!" we say to encourage someone who hurts. Even non-Christians think this way—"She has such faith"—without stopping to consider what the person has faith *in*. (The object of faith is even more important than faith itself.)

If a person who perseveres and maintains hope has faith, what does the person who loses hope have? That is, what is the opposite of faith? A quick response might be "doubt"—and for good reason. One who doubts is certainly experiencing the erosion of faith.

But there are good reasons to think that the complete opposite of faith is not doubt, but fear. Which brings us to the third reason we win in the end: Because I know the love of God in Christ, I should never be afraid of anything.

Why is fear the opposite of faith? The answer is because both have to do with the future. Recall the story of Jesus and His disciples traveling across the Sea of Galilee in a fishing boat (Mark 4:35–41). Jesus went to the rear of the boat and fell asleep while the disciples manned the sails. As still can happen on the Sea of Galilee today, a violent storm suddenly arose. The huge waves crashed over them, filling the boat with water, threatening to sink it. The disciples woke Jesus and implored Him to do something—which He did. He rebuked the wind and ordered the sea to be at peace. Then He asked the disciples a telling question: "Why are you so afraid? Have you still no faith?"

When you are traveling from one side of a large body of

water to the other, the future is always in question. In the simplest of terms, there can be only two outcomes: You will make it to the other side or you will not. It is in the midst of the journey that things happen that elicit either faith or fear. Doubt arises when storm clouds gather, but it is fear—stark terror when you realize you might not make it—that comes forth when the gale actually hits. Consider it in Titanic terms: Faith was when you purchased your ticket on an unsinkable ship; doubt set in when the iceberg was struck; fear was what gripped you when you realized you had trusted in something that could not deliver.

The future is not debatable; its approach is not an option. The question is not whether we face an unknown future—we do. The question is whether we will approach that future with faith or with fear. Unfortunately, some Christians live as if they are entering the future alone. They don't mean to live that way any more than the disciples planned to be overcome with fear on the Sea of Galilee. The disciples were just as fearful with Jesus in the boat as they would have been had He been a hundred miles away. They lived their lives that day as if His presence in their boat was not a factor in their future. That is where we also can make a serious mistake—living our lives as if Jesus Christ were not in the boat with us.

The apostle Paul said he was certain—literally he said, "I have been convinced"—that nothing in his future could prevent him from arriving at the destination God had planned for him (see Romans 8:29). Paul feared no thing, no man, no angel, nothing in the present or the future; not death and not life. Paul was not afraid of anything because he walked by faith, not by fear.

I hope as you have meditated on what Paul wrote in Romans 8 that you also have been convinced not to fear anything. Regardless of your circumstances today or tomorrow, you have no reason not to have hope if you are walking with Christ. And if you are not walking with Christ, wouldn't today be a good day to begin? The only way to be free of fear is to be full of faith in Him.

CONCLUSION
Supernatural Hope

Moments in time that mark history forever also leave a lasting impact on our emotions. I may be sitting in a packed stadium cheering for my favorite team or casually walking through the mall with my wife, Deb, and I catch myself looking into the faces of the people around me and wondering: *Is that individual a hero or heroine?* I wonder if anyone in this crowd has the strength and courage to rise to the occasion and perform a heroic deed?

I don't think any one of us can predict accurately just how we would respond in a time of crisis. We may be intellectually equipped or trained; however, circumstances can affect our reactions.

I have been called to the bedside of many individuals suffering or severely injured, and by God's grace I can touch the individual, pray with compassion, and reach out to family members to comfort them. However, when Deb or one of my kids or grandkids is hurt or sick, I don't have the same emotional strength. I know the reality of the situation, but my heart and head don't work in concert. My heart takes over, and it is difficult to think rationally.

Physical tragedy brings pain and suffering, but we must keep in perspective the reality pointed out in Luke 12:4–5: We should not fear what may kill our bodies, but we should fear the One who can kill our souls.

As believers in the Lord Jesus Christ, we need to demonstrate courage and boldly tell the message of salvation that is possible through a personal relationship with Jesus.

True heroes and heroines protect, rescue, and defend. When someone is threatened by impending danger, our bodies have an amazing capacity to respond. We've read accounts of individuals who have moved heavy objects with Herculean strength to free a trapped person. The surge of adrenaline at the time of crisis allows us to respond with unnatural power.

For the Christian, there is a supernatural strength that can empower every believer. The Spirit of God will empower you to bring hope to the hopeless, joy to the joyless, courage to the fearful, and strength to the weary.

Just think of it, we have been given the gift of supernatural hope for a future in eternity ... and the future starts now.

Then I saw a new heaven and a new earth, for the first heaven and the first earth had passed away, and the sea was no more. And I saw the holy city, new Jerusalem, coming down out of heaven from God, prepared as a bride adorned for her husband. And I heard a loud voice from the throne saying, "Behold, the dwelling place of God is with man. He will dwell with them, and they will be his people, and God himself will be with them as their God. He will wipe away every tear from their eyes, and death shall be no more, neither shall there be mourning, nor crying, nor pain anymore, for the former things have passed away." —Revelation 21:1–4

Please call 1-800-414-7693 or visit jackgraham.org/store to order the following products:

BOOKS:

Lord, Hear our Cry
New Life in Christ
Breaking Free From Addiction
You Can Make a Difference
God's Promises for Doubt-filled days
Lifebook:The Authority, Authenticity and Accuracy of God's Word A Man of God
Are You Fit for Life?
Life According to Jesus
Powering Up
CultureWise
Marriage by the Book
Unseen: Angels, Satan, Heaven, Hell, and Winning the Battle for Eternity

DEVOTIONALS:

A Daily Encounter with God

GRAHAM
1-800-414-7693
jgraham@powerpoint.org
www.jackgraham.org